The Life of
St David

Please return/renew this item
by the last date shown.
Books may also be renewed by
phone and Internet.

www.heinemann.co.uk/library
Visit our website to find out more information about **Heinemann Library** books.

To order:
 Phone 44 (0) 1865 888066
 Send a fax to 44 (0) 1865 314091
 Visit the Heinemann Bookshop at www.heinemann.co.uk/library to browse our catalogue and order online.

First published in Great Britain by Heinemann Library, Halley Court, Jordan Hill, Oxford OX2 8EJ, part of Harcourt Education.
Heinemann is a registered trademark of Harcourt Education Ltd.

Editorial: Lucy Thunder and Helen Cannons
Design: Richard Parker and Tinstar Design Ltd. (www.tinstar.co.uk)
Illustrations: Maureen Gray
Picture Research: Rebecca Sodergren and Liz Moore
Production: Edward Moore

Originated by Repro Multi-Warna
Printed and bound in China by South China Printing Company
The paper used to print this book comes from sustainable resources.

ISBN 0 431 18081 4
08 07 06 05
10 9 8 7 6 5 4 3 2

British Library Cataloguing in Publication Data
Anita Ganeri
The Life of St David. – (Life of saints)
270.2'092
A full catalogue record for this book is available from the British Library.

Acknowledgements
The publishers would like to thank the following for permission to reproduce photographs: Collections **p 6**; Collections/Philip Craven **p 7**; Collections/Lawrence Englesberg **p 15**; Collections/Robert Hallman **p 23**; Collections/David Mansell **p 21**; Collections/Michael St Maur Sheil **p 26**; Collections/George Wright **p 9**; Corbis UK Ltd/Macdufff Everton **p 22**; E & E Picture Library/R. Pilgrim **p 14**; Fortean Picture Library/Janet and Colin Bord **p 20**; Robert Harding Picture Library/Simon Harris **p 16**; Jeff Moore **p 18**; Picture Library Wales **pp 10, 24, 25, 27**; Topham Picturepoint/ImageWorks **p 4**; Trip/J Highet **p 13**; Trip/H. Rogers **p 5**.

Cover photograph of St David, on a stained-glass window, reproduced with permission of The Photo Library Wales.

The publishers would like to thank Fr. Martin Ganeri OP for his assistance in the preparation of this book.

Every effort has been made to contact copyright holders of any material reproduced in this book. Any omissions will be rectified in subsequent printings if notice is given to the publishers.

Contents

Words shown in the text in bold, **like this**, are explained in the glossary.

What is a saint?

In the **Christian** religion, people try to live a **holy** life. Some men and women are especially holy. The Christian Church calls them saints. Christians believe that saints are very close to God.

Some Christians pray to the saints to help them.

Some saints look after a country or a group of people, such as doctors or travellers. They are called **patron saints**. This book is about St David, the patron saint of Wales.

St David is usually shown dressed in robes with a long beard, as he is here.

St David's parents

David was born over 1500 years ago in south-west Wales. We do not know much for certain about David's life. Most of our information comes from stories and legends.

David was born here, on the Pembrokeshire coast in south-west Wales.

Legend says that David's father was a **chief**, called Prince Sant. His mother was a **holy** woman, called Lady Non or Nonna. She was the daughter of a chief.

The **Chapel** of St Nun, at St David's in Wales, is named after David's mother.

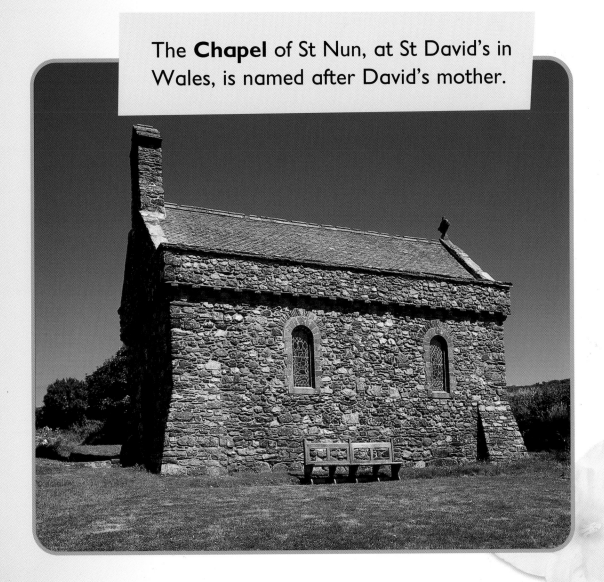

A special baby

Before David was born, his mother went into a church. When the priest saw her, he found that he could not speak. This was a sign that she was going to have a special baby.

Another amazing thing happened when David was **baptized**. **Holy water** was sprinkled on his head. Some of the water splashed on a blind man's face and he could see again.

Holy water is kept in fonts, like this one. Holy water is used for baptizing babies.

Becoming a monk

When David grew up, he decided to become a **monk**. He travelled to a **monastery** in Wales to study. His teacher was an old blind monk, called Paulinus.

These are the remains of the Welsh monastery where David studied.

David stayed at the monastery for ten years. He was famous for his **holy** powers. Legend says that he gave Paulinus back his sight by making the sign of the cross.

David goes on his travels

One night, Paulinus saw an angel in his dreams. The angel told him to send David to teach people to be **Christians**. So David set off on his travels with two other **monks**.

David travelled far and wide. He went to England, France and Ireland. In England, David visited the great **abbey** at Glastonbury in Somerset. Here he built a new **chapel**.

Glastonbury Abbey in Somerset, England.

A great monastery

David's travels also took him all over Wales. He was very kind and gentle and lots of people came to listen to him. Many of them became **Christians** after hearing David teach.

David is often shown in pictures with a book in his hand, looking wise.

David built a great **monastery** on the banks of a river. This is where the tiny city of St David's stands today. David lived in this monastery with his **monks**.

Today, many churches in Wales are named after David, like this one.

A very hard life

David and his **monks** lived a strict, hard life. Most of the time they did not speak. They had only bread, salt and vegetables to eat. They drank and washed in cold water from the river.

David and his monks fetched water from the river near their **monastery**.

Every morning, the monks got up early
for prayers. Afterwards, they had to
work very hard ploughing the fields
and looking after the crops they grew.

David's life in danger

There are many stories about David's life. One tells how David's enemies tried to kill him. They gave him some **poisoned** bread to eat.

This is the type of bread that monks might have eaten in the 6th century.

18

An Irish **monk** called Scuthyn heard of the wicked plot. He rode from Ireland on a sea monster and told David. Then David **blessed** the bread and ate it without being harmed.

An amazing meeting

Once, David was asked to talk to a meeting of **Christians** in Wales. Thousands of people came along. But they were worried they would not be able to see or hear David clearly.

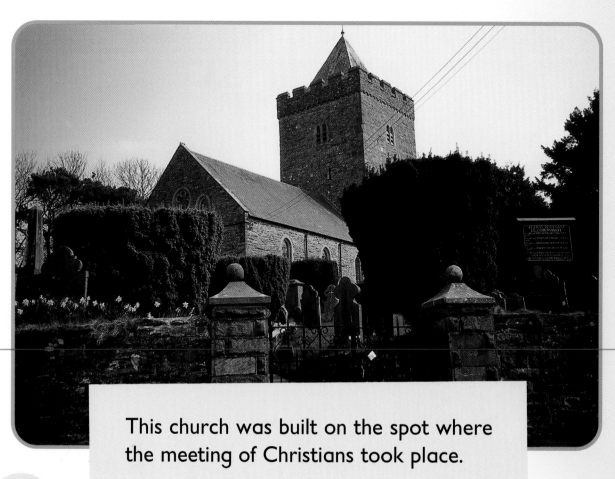

This church was built on the spot where the meeting of Christians took place.

Legend says that, as David was speaking, the ground rose up beneath his feet. It made a hill for David to stand on so that he could be seen and heard by everyone.

Another legend says that a dove landed on David's shoulder. It was a sign of God.

21

David dies

After this meeting, David was chosen to be **Archbishop** of Wales. He became the leader of the Welsh **Christians**. Many people came to visit him at his **monastery** in St David's.

The tiny city of St David's in Wales.

When he was over 100 years old, David died in his monastery. A story says that the monastery was filled with angels who carried his soul up to heaven.

Later a great **cathedral** was built where the monastery once stood.

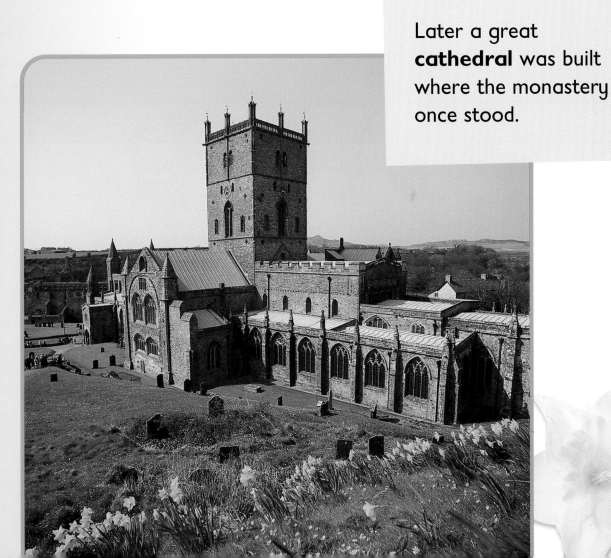

St David of Wales

David was buried in the grounds of his **monastery**. This is where St David's **Cathedral** now stands. About 500 years after his death, David was chosen to be **patron saint** of Wales.

David was buried in this tomb in St David's Cathedral.

Legend says there was once a battle between the Welsh and the **Saxons**. David told the Welsh soldiers to wear leeks in their hats to tell them apart from their enemies.

Leeks are worn on St David's Day to celebrate the story of the battle.

St David's Day

On 1 March, people all over the world celebrate St David's Day. To mark the day, Welsh people pin leeks or daffodils to their clothes.

These girls are dressed up in colourful costumes for a St David's Day parade.

There are also festivals of singing and dancing. These are called eisteddfods. People read poetry in the Welsh language. Some people dress up in their Welsh costumes.

This choir is singing at an eisteddfod to celebrate St David's Day.

Fact file

- In pictures and statues, St David is usually shown dressed as a **bishop**, with a long beard. He stands on a hill, with a dove perched on his shoulder. The dove is a sign of God.

- In the Welsh language, St David is called *Dewi* or *Dafydd*.

- St David's nickname is 'The Water Drinker' because he only ever drank water. Legend says that wherever David went a spring of water gushed out of the ground.

- St David's **Cathedral** is the biggest cathedral in Wales. But there are also 50 other churches of St David in Wales.

Timeline

The first story of St David's life was written about 500 years after he died. We do not know how much of it is true and how much is legend. We do not know for certain when St David was born or died. You can use the dates below as a guide.

- **Around AD 487** St David is born in south-west Wales
- **Around 545** St David talks to a meeting of **Christians**. A **miracle** happens and a hill rises up under his feet.
- **Around 589** St David dies on 1 March. He is over 100 years old. Some people think that he lived even longer than that and died when he was 147 years old.
- **Around 1090** The first story of St David's life is written
- **Around 1120** David is made a saint by Pope Callistus II. He becomes **patron saint** of Wales.
- **Around 1398** St David's Day is celebrated for the first time

Glossary

abbey building like a monastery

AD way of counting dates, starting from year zero

archbishop senior bishop or leader in the Christian Church

baptized when a person joins the Christian Church. They are sprinkled with or dipped in holy water at a special service.

bishop leader in the Christian church

blessed to make someone or something holy

cathedral large church

chapel small church or part of a church

chief leader of a group or head of a family

Christians people who follow the teachings of Jesus Christ

holy to do with God

holy water water that has been blessed

miracle event which shows God's special power

monastery building where monks live

monk man who belongs to a special religious group

patron saint saint who has a special interest in a country or a group of people

poisoned made bad by adding poison

Saxons people who invaded Britain in the 5th century AD

Find out more

Books

Celebrations!: Christmas, Jennifer Gillis (Raintree, 2003)

Places of Worship: Catholic Churches, Clare Richards (Heinemann Library, 1999)

Places of Worship: Protestant Churches, Mandy Ross (Heinemann Library, 1999)

Websites

www.britainexpress.com
Information about different parts of Britain, the history of Britain and famous people, including saints.

www.stdavidscathedral.org.uk
The website of St David's Cathedral in Wales. It gives lots of information about the cathedral and its history.

Index

Titles in *The Life of* series include:

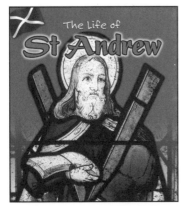

Hardback   0 431 18084 9

Hardback   0 431 18081 4

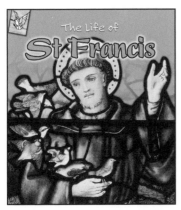

Hardback   0 431 18080 6

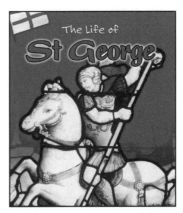

Hardback   0 431 18082 2

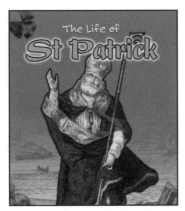

Hardback   0 431 18083 0

Find out about the other titles in this series on our website www.heinemann.co.uk/library